SO-CGQ-264

GOD LISTENS
to Your Care

GOD LISTENS
to Your Care

PRAYERS FOR ALL THE ANIMALS OF THE WORLD

CAROL J. ADAMS

THE PILGRIM PRESS   CLEVELAND

IN HONOR OF ALL THE ANIMALS

WHO TOUCH OUR LIVES AND NEED OUR CARE

The Pilgrim Press, 700 Prospect Avenue, Cleveland, Ohio 44115-1100
thepilgrimpress.com
Copyright © 2006 Carol J. Adams

All rights reserved. Published 2006

Printed in the United States of America on acid-free paper

10   09   08   07   06   5   4   3   2   1

Library of Congress Cataloging-in-Publication Data

Adams, Carol J.
    God listens to your care : prayers for all the animals of the world /
    Carol J. Adams.
        p. cm.—(God listens)
        ISBN 0-8298-1666-6
        1. Prayers for animals—Juvenile literature.   2. Pet owners—Prayer-books and
devotions—English—Juvenile literature.   I. Title.

BV283.A63A318 2006
242'.82—dc22

                                                            2005028966

CONTENTS

Dear Friend,

I cannot remember a time when I was not aware of animals. Is this true for you, too? Do you notice animals wherever you go and think of animals you learn about though you have never seen them? Have you always been aware of the animals nearby and the animals far away? Of the animals who live in the sea, the forests, the jungles, the oceans, and on farms?

Or are you beginning to notice the other animals and are amazed by all the feelings that caring for animals awakens within you?

I wrote these prayers because of my awareness of the other animals.

But I did not write these prayers only because I am aware of animals. I wrote these prayers because I am also aware of God's presence in my life and the lives of the animals.

When I walk near a pond and hear ducks quacking, see turtles basking in the sun, watch a goose honk at baby ducklings she is helping to take care of, when I see squirrels scamper across the grass and up a cottonwood tree, when I experience the pond and the life that is being lived there, it is then that I feel God's presence.

The animals make me aware of God.

Whatever we are feeling—awe or doubt, happiness or sadness, joy or worry—we can share these feelings with God. We can bring our concerns to God, concerns about ourselves, but also concerns about the other animals.

When we are aware of animals we become open to very powerful feelings—awe and joy, but also worry and sadness. Because these feelings are so powerful, it is good to share them with God.

If there is a prayer for an animal you wish I had included, or a prayer about your feelings for animals that you wish would be written, please let me know. You can write to me care of The Pilgrim Press, 700 Prospect Avenue, Cleveland, OH 44115-1100, or by email to cja@caroljadams.com.

Dear friend, you are not alone in caring about animals. God listens to your care.

God, have you made me a little Noah to help the animals

    on the ark that is this world?

Help me protect the animals,

    on the ark that is this world

Help me educate others

    on the ark that is this world.

Help us work together

    on the ark that is this world.

God, this time around we all need to be Noahs,

    don't we?

Noahs on the ark that is this world.

Dear God,

I like thinking of the animals.

I like saying their names; they are so different.

My alphabet of animals could be:

Aardvarks, bats, cats,

dogs, elephants, frogs,

gerbils, horses, impalas,

jaguars, kangaroos, leopards.

Mink, narwhals, opossums,

pigeons, quetzals, rabbits,

sloths, tigers, umbrella birds,

vervets, wolves, yaks, zebras.

Or it could be:

Zokors, yellowhammers, woodchucks,

vicunas, unicorns, tapirs,

sheep, raccoons, quail,

    porpoises, otters, newts,

monkeys, lions, koalas,

    jackals, ibex, hippopotamuses,

groundhogs, fox, eland, deer,

    camels, bears, anteaters.

There are so many others I could name!

And when I say each name,

I think: please be with them.

A to Z and back again, be with them.

God, how wonderful your world is.

I wonder how you created elephants.

> They are so big.

> Their trunks swing.

> They are nothing like me—

>> isn't that wonderful!

I wonder how you created porcupines.

> They walk on four legs.

> Their quills are their armor.

> They are nothing like me—

>> isn't that wonderful!

I wonder how you created the birds.

> Their winged flight over my head invites me

>> to look at your vast sky.

> I know they are descendants of the dinosaurs—

>> that amazes me.

They are nothing like me—

    isn't that wonderful!

But, God of wonder,

    I do see that elephants are like me

    and so are the porcupines

    and so are the birds—and all animals.

We were all created by you.

That is so wonderful!

God bless the animals I know.

God bless the animals I have met.

God bless the animals who live

with my friends.

God bless the animals who live

in this town.

God bless the animals who live

in this country.

God bless the animals who live

on this continent.

God bless the animals who live

in this hemisphere.

God bless the animals who live

in this world.

God bless the animals

we don't even know exist.

God bless the animals who

were sent to circle the heavens

in spaceships, never to return.

God bless all the animals

who are with you in heaven.

Amen.

God, thank you for this morning.

Thank you for birds singing morning songs.

Thank you for all the nighttime animals

    who made it through the night,

        including me.

Thank you for the daytime animals

    who are beginning their day,

        including me.

Be with all your creatures this day,

    O Holy One,

        including me.

Dear God,

Thank you for caterpillars.

 Do they know who they will become?

Thank you for their cocoons.

 When someone is changing,

 You can't always see it—the becoming.

Thank you for butterflies.

 Your very own kaleidoscope.

One fluttered by today.

The wings seemed to wave hello.

How many different ways there are to be in the world!

Dear God, O Holy One,

Today I saw a dead squirrel in the street.

It made me feel sad.

I thought I saw his tail move.

When I think of the squirrel,

I think of scampering,

    running, tree-climbing,

    branch-clinging, limb-leaping,

    nut-hunting squirrels,

not dead ones immobile on the street.

Thank you for each squirrel's energy.

Thank you for all the different kinds and colors

    of squirrels.

This one did not survive.

God, help the acrobats of the backyard

    when they dart through traffic.

Help them become the winners

    of the street-crossing dash.

Not the losers of life to cars

    that barely note their passing.

I mourn this one's death.

Comfort me, O Holy One.

Dear God,

Thank you for the pond.

A swallow flies above it.

A waterbug skims on top.

A frog leaps from the bank when I get too near.

Tadpoles slither away.

Egg sacs nestle in the weeds.

Minnows swish by.

God, if I didn't get close,

    I'd miss it all.

I'd skim over the surface,

    like the waterbug.

So much is happening—

    each part of the pond is connected

    to the other in a jigsaw

whose pattern is realized

underneath the water.

God, I am grateful I could get so close

and see things I often pass unnoticing.

I am grateful I am part of the pattern,

Even if I can't see all of it:

The flying, skimming, swimming,

leaping, slithering,

walking, swishing, seeing world.

Thank you for my part in it.

Dear God,

I've been thinking about dinosaurs.

Why did they have to go extinct?

I wish I could see just one.

Couldn't you make that happen?

Just one? For me?

I don't think I would ever ask for much more than that.

Why did they go extinct, God?

That worries me.

If they—who ruled the world—could all die out,

    does that mean we could too?

They were so huge, some of them,

    and then they died out.

We're not big like them.

We're not strong like them.

They were so fast, some of them.

And at least one of them had two brains!

Were some of them smarter than we are?

Yet they all died out,

> the huge and the small,

> the fast and the slow,

> those with two brains

> and those with only one.

I guess I do have something else to ask for:

God, I hope we don't die out like that.

World-creators in webs and dirt;

many-legged and no-legged;

surveyors of life at ground level

    and below—

I love your smallness.

How complete you are.

My inches are your miles.

I pray your world is not my

    inconvenience.

I worry where I step.

I don't want to crush a friend.

I pray my world has room for you.

Dear God,

I saw a homeless man downtown today.

He had a dog on a rope.

They were walking together.

Both looked dirty and thin.

But both looked happy together.

I saw a shopping bag lady with a

cat sticking out of her push basket.

A friend told me about a homeless girl who

had a bunny for a friend,

and about a boy with a pet rat,

and another with a snake.

I pray for homeless animals

and the people who struggle to keep

them safe and fed even

when they are having a tough time

keeping themselves healthy and whole.

Dear God,

Today we saw a dog running by the road.

No one was near the dog.

I am so worried about this dog.

Is she still safe?

So many cars were rushing by.

I was scared that the dog would be hit.

God, we passed by that dog.

At times when I have felt lost and alone

I was glad special friends did not pass me by.

Please, God, don't pass by.

Be here with me and

be with that dog.

Keep us both safe.

Animal shelters always need your support. They need towels and food and other supplies too, as well as volunteer help. You and your family can contact your nearest animal shelter and ask them about how you can help them.

Today, God, I like to think that

I was your arms as I took

    old towels to the animal shelter.

I could hear all the animals who are there.

Many seemed to be happy to see me.

They all seemed to cry out, "Take me home."

"I'll be your friend."

Keep them safe, God.

Keep them warm and dry.

May my towels keep you near to them.

May my act keep you near to me.

Sometimes school work includes reading books like Where the Red Fern Grows, Old Yeller, *and other books that include the death of animals. This can be very upsetting. Here is a prayer you can say if you have to read a book like this.*

I had to read a book in school, God, that upset me.

It included the death of an animal.

I felt mad, God,

    mad because of what happened to the animal.

And I felt sad, too,

    sad because I had to read about it.

I felt mad because my teacher

    had assigned the book.

And sad because I didn't know

    what was going to happen,

    and then it happened.

You are the God of words, O God.

I wish those words had not hurt me.

I wish I wasn't reminded that animals die like that.

But you have given me words, too, God,

and with them I can speak my mind.

May my real words keep real animals alive and well.

Dear God,

Today my class went to the zoo.

Everyone was excited.

We saw many different types of animals, God.

Someone said the zoo was like Noah's ark.

But God, Noah's animals were set free.

Loving God, today I saw what "captive" means.

All of those wonderful animals that you created
were not free.

But they told us the animals were safe and live longer
in the zoo.

But do zoos make animals happy?

I am worried about those animals, God.

Noah brought the animals into the ark to save them,
not to show them off.

I feel sad for the animals I saw.

Be with them and be with me.

Dear God,

People have walking paths in parks

　　to stretch and run on,

　　pools to swim and dive in,

　　playgrounds to swing on

　　and monkey bars to hang from.

I pray for the day that those animals

　　who have legs are able to walk,

　　able even to run, if they wish

that animals who have fins are able to swim,

　　wherever they wish to go,

that animals who have wings are able to fly,

　　able to stretch, when they wish.

I don't wish for that day.

I pray for that day.

God, I like to have a walking prayer.

I like to look up into the trees and think—

    may you animals whom I can't see,

    up in those limbs,

    may you animals be safe.

And I like to look at the ground and think—

    may you animals whom I can't see,

    down under the ground,

    may you animals be safe.

And I like to look at the sidewalks and find slug trails

    and think—

    may you who leave trails

    that glisten and shine like glass,

    may you be safe.

And as I keep walking, I look up at the sky;

    I look at the trees;

    I look at the ground;

    I look at the sidewalk.

And I think—

    may you, God,

    you whom I can't see,

    may you keep all your animals safe.

Dear God,

I heard on the news today about an animal in trouble.

I am worried about this.

Why has this happened?

God, I am so far away from this animal.

I cannot save this animal by reaching out my arms

　　in rescue.

But I can do this.

I can pray for this animal's safety.

So please, God, keep this animal safe.

Dear God,

I saw a poster on a pole nearby.

It had a picture of a lost animal friend

    whose family is looking for her.

They are asking for help.

Aren't you the God of four-footed animals, too?

I am worried for this animal.

    Is she injured? Is she lost?

    Is she all alone?

I am worried for her family;

    they must be scared.

    I know that's how I would feel.

God, right now there are many of us who feel worried

    and sad.

Give us a hug, God.

Please, God, be with the lost one.

Please, God, guide her back home to her family.

Dear God,

Today there was a bird at my window

    bringing the news of the day.

The bird seemed to say:

    "Look outside!"

    "If you could have seen all that I saw

      as I flew over here!"

    "Consider all that is possible!"

When the bird flew away,

    my thoughts flew away, too,

    though I stayed at my window.

I was thinking:

Who says the animals don't have a voice?

Who says this world was made for us?

I was still inside

    looking out my window.

But the bird was crossing territory

    I'll never see.

I pray tomorrow that a bird

    might come to my window again

    to bring me news of the day

    and perhaps point the way.

"I'm listening!" I want to say.

God, I'm listening.

Listening to voices that don't use words.

Dear God,

When it comes to farm animals,

    It feels that I have always been told otherwise.

Cows and their calves don't swish their tails together,

    down on the farm.

    It is otherwise.

Chickens don't scratch and peck and cluck,

    and sit on their own roost,

    down on the farm.

    It is otherwise.

Pigs aren't rooting and nuzzling

    and enjoying mud baths

    down on the farm

    It is otherwise.

They hardly are allowed to move at all:

> Chickens in cages, six to a cage.

> Calves don't stay with their mothers.

> Pigs in crates.

I wish it were otherwise.

Dear God, I wish I had known the truth.

> It seems we are letting the farm animals down.

> It seems we are letting you down.

> I wish it were otherwise.

God, if you are all-powerful,

    why did you let the dodo die?

    Not only the dodo, the passenger pigeon.

Thousands of species have already vanished—

    three species every hour!

    How can you let this happen?

I try to imagine how you could stop this.

Maybe you could stop time and give us all

    a second chance.

But you would have to stop so many people.

    Not only the person who

        killed the last dodo,

    but the people who

        started killing the first dodo.

    Not only the person who

        killed the last passenger pigeon,

but the people who

started shooting the first ones.

God, how did people let them die?

How are we letting them die, now?

Is there something that I am doing that makes

me one of the people who is helping

to kill a species?

God, what power we human beings have!

Is that your answer?

Am I part of your answer?

It is up to us?

God, help me make a difference.

Dear God,

It seems unbelievable

    that the ivory-billed woodpecker

    has reappeared.

Until recently, sixty years had gone by

    and not a single one had been seen.

Sixty years is a long time, God.

Were they hiding from people who can

    hurt and hunt them?

No wonder people thought this woodpecker was extinct.

It makes me think of other animals

    who might be hiding from us.

The Loch Ness Monster.

Bigfoot.

The Jersey Devil.

Maybe they are shy.

Maybe they are afraid.

Maybe they were hurt and threatened

and want to be left alone.

God, I am thankful that woodpecker survived,

and that we got a peek at her.

And yet, if the ivory-billed woodpecker,

Why not the others?

Might they be out there somewhere?

Dear God,

I am thankful for my home, my living space:

>Where I play and where I eat,

>where I enjoy my family

>>and where I see my friends.

I feel safe and don't fear tomorrow.

God, so many homes of animals are threatened:

>Where they play and where they eat,

>where they enjoy their families

>>and where they see their friends.

They may not live in too many tomorrows.

If we take away their homes,

>we destroy so much more, too.

How can they survive?

God, I pray for the black-footed ferret,

>who needs the prairie to live in.

But prairies are disappearing.

As are birds.

I like to think of the black-footed ferret because

   it is easier to focus on one species.

As for birds, 252 different bird species

   are threatened throughout the world.

Not only birds,

not only the black-footed ferret—

God, please help endangered animals.

Help us, too, God.

Help us love *their* homes as

   much as we love our own;

to respect *their* needs

   as much as we do our own.

I know I am asking a lot.

But I don't ask it for myself, alone . . .

I ask it for the black-footed ferret

 and for the 252 bird species

 and for all the animals.

May we help them live.

Dear God,

My prayer is simple.

> May we care for animals.

My prayer is simple,

and I will say it again:

> May we care for animals.

I could say it a different way:

> May we care about what is happening to animals,

I could say it pointedly:

> May we care enough to help them.

My prayer is simple,

> but I know it asks that we human beings change.

My prayer is urgent:

> May we care enough to change.

Dear God,

who will answer my prayer?

> May we care for animals.

Baaa.

Whippoorwill.

Cluck.

Moo.

Hee haw.

Gobble gobble.

Caw.

Meow.

Oink.

Cock-a-doodle-doo.

Ribbit.

Tweet tweet tweet.

Quack quack.

Coo.

Tu-whit. Tu-whit.

Alleluia.